Contant

MEI GIRLS × 2020

蕾拉

Lyla

instagram： @la.112814

偽裝的生活有點膩，
真實的生活有點甜。

Pink Dream

2020

Taiwan

Top 100 Girls Album

MEI GIRLS × 2020

Lyla

MEI
GIRLS
×
2020
Lyla
Sweet
Fantasy
I long to be a sunflower
a lover of golden light,
a creator of sweet laughter.

Pretty In Pink

2020
Taiwan
Top 100 Girls Album

MEI GIRLS

2020

美麗妄娜

instagram： @wanna10_4

「不怕黑只怕不紅，
不怕不紅只怕不夠真。」

MEI GIRLS
2020

MEI GIRLS 2020

-

Shine Your Light

Blossom Forest

You'll silently bloom,
Beautifully in your own way

-

Shine Your Light

MEI
GIRLS
×
2020
You'll silently bloom,
Beautifully in your own way

MEI GIRLS × 2020

李小星

DJ Xin

instagram： @djxin_tw

「我不是不喜歡這個世界，
而是我只喜歡有你的世界。」

MEI GIRLS 2020

Be My Star

2020
Taiwan
Top 100 Girls Album

Cheetos
15

Cheetos
15

MEI GIRLS
2020
DJ Xin

SUM —
MER
2 0 2 0

Let Me Shine For You

You are made
Of stars

2020
Taiwan Top 100 Girls Album

「保持善良，莫忘初心。」

MEI GIRLS × 2020

采瑄

Ning

instagram： @cutening0976

Classic
Beauty
I'm happy
When I'm with you
2020
Taiwan Top 100 Girls Album

MEI
GIRLS
×
2020
Ning

-

***Closer To Happiness
Than I've Ever Been***

2020
Taiwan Top 100 Girls Album

Love Finds You

-

Closer To Happiness
Than I've Ever Been

MEI GIRLS × 2020

啾啾
吳慈敏

instagram： @chuchu0526

「別人都是小仙女，
我是你永遠都得不到的爹。」

[打開你的心，我想住一輩子♥]

MEI GIRLS × 2020

蔡譯心

Candice

instagram： @candice0723

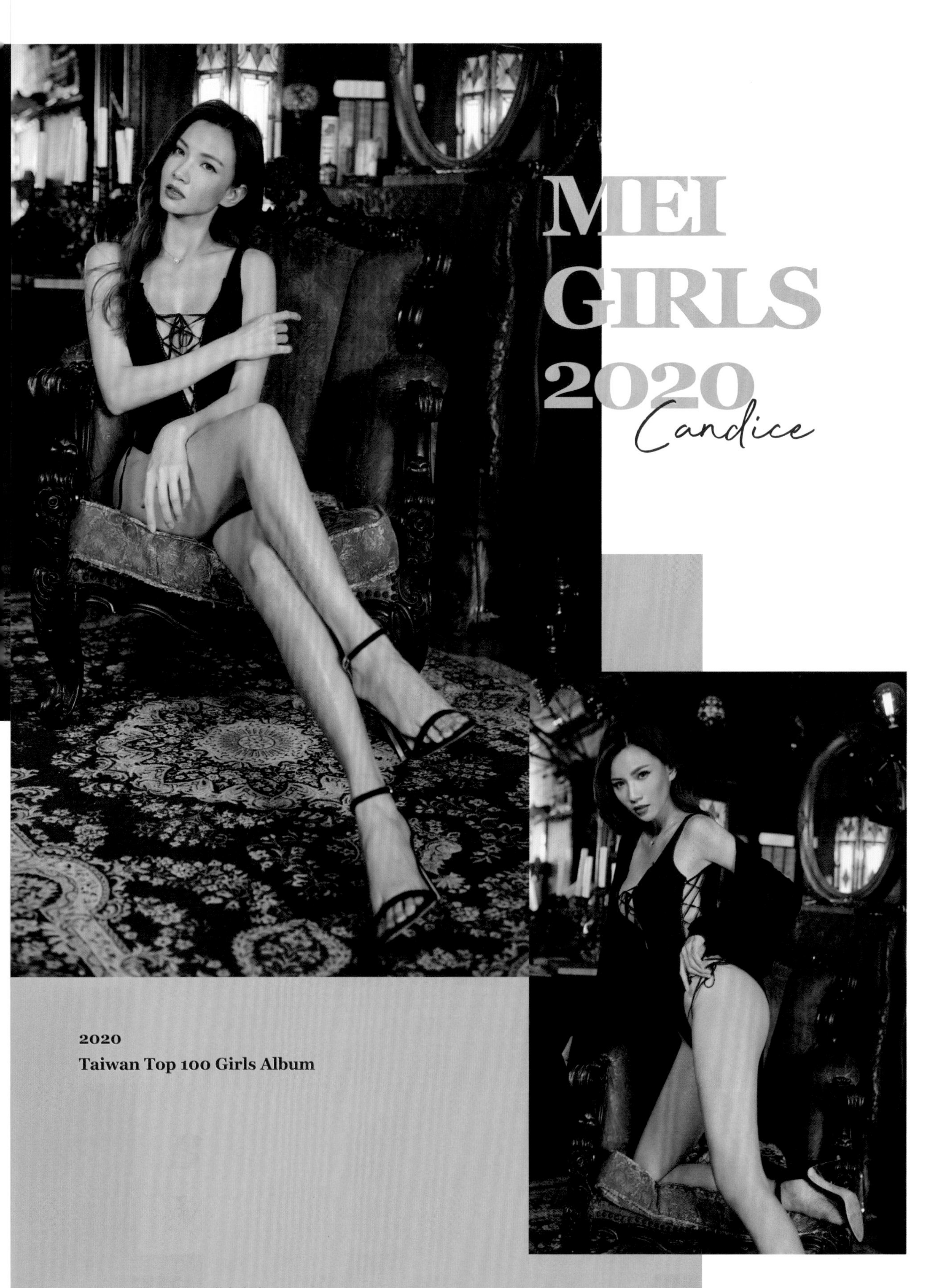
MEI
GIRLS
2020
Candice
2020
Taiwan Top 100 Girls Album

Best Memories

Take my hand and
my whole life too.
I can't help falling in love
with you

MEI GIRLS × 2020

李馨

Cin Cin

instagram： @cin_cin_li

賞月，賞花，賞馨馨

MEI GIRLS 2020

Cin Cin

Waking Up
To
The Sound
Of Love

2020 Taiwan Top 100 Girls Album

Wake Me Up

I fell for you
And I am still falling

MEI GIRLS × 2020

李花

Fa Fa

instagram： @fafaa728

「我死後請把我ㄉ骨灰撒進大海，
我掛ㄉ也得繼續浪」

MEI GIRLS 2020

Fa Fa

2 0 2 0

Sum

- mer

Cozy Vibes

Belong with you ,
Belong with me

2
0
2
0

2020
Taiwan Top 100 Girls Album

MEI GIRLS × 2020

青青

instagram： @c.0214

[青青給你親親❤]

MEI GIRLS 2020

#XOXO

2020
Taiwan
Top 100 Girls
Album.

MEI GIRLS 2020

Summertime

Life Is Made Of Small Moments Like This

S'dare Sport
SPORTHOLIC

#XOXO

2020
Taiwan
Top 100 Girls
Album.

MEI GIRLS 2020

-

Dream
A Little Dream
Of Me

You Are My Adventure

Closer to happiness than I've ever been

MEI GIRLS 2020

Taiwan Top 100 Girls Album.

Best Memories

Shining Day

MEI GIRLS 2020

Taiwan Top 100 Girls Album.

Daydream

The best thing to hold onto in life is each other.

MEI GIRLS × 2020

安琪

Angel

instagram： @anchi916

「可愛只是兩個字，卻跟了我一生一世。」

summertime

Breezy Summer Day

Dream a little dream of me

MEI GIRLS 2020

Angel

Taiwan Top 100 Girls Album.

summertime

MEI GIRLS × 2020

潔西

Jessie

instagram：@sheep_tsai

別的女孩都迷人，
我不一樣，我磨人。

Taiwan Top 100 Girls
Album.

Jessie

MEI GIRLS 2020

Jessie

Summer Vibes

-

In your life
my infinite dreams live.

All Of Me Loves All Of You

Dream a little dream of me

Taiwan Top 100 Girls Album.

Be
Happy
Always
Artemis

MEI GIRLS × 2020

子珊

Freya

instagram： @tzushan520_

好好生活，慢慢愛你，
不早不晚，剛好是你。

這世界很煩，但我要很可愛❤

MEI GIRLS × 2020

柯姿

KZi

instagram： @kziiee

MEI GIRLS × 2020

KZi

Be My Star
YOU
ARE BETTER
THAN
ALL
ANYTHING!

MEI GIRLS × 2020

Salen

instagram： @salen_wu

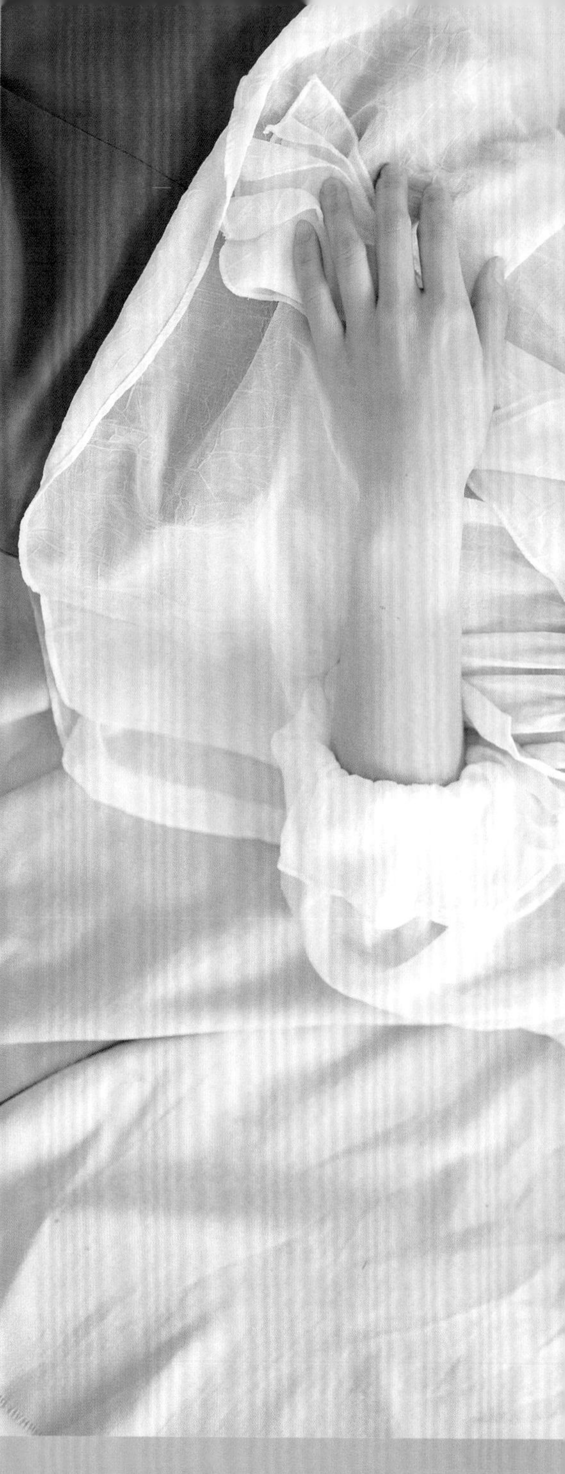

不用再問我都飛什麼線，
因為我飛的都叫理智線。

Taiwan Top 100 Girls Album.

2 0 2 0
Sum
- mer

Dream A Little Dream Of Me

Your smile is a blessing

Let Me Shine For You

-

The best thing to hold onto in life is each other.

MEI GIRLS 2020

Juby

MEI GIRLS

2020

小筑

Nina

instagram： @changyachuu

最近心不在焉，因為心在你那邊♥

-
Life is made of
small moments
like this
Love In
Your
Heart

MEI GIRLS 2020

Nina

Taiwan
Top 100 Girls Album.

Be Happy Always

-

Wish some days lasted forever

Be
Happy
Always

MEI GIRLS × 2020

-

Wish some days lasted forever

生命中的不期而遇
都是你努力的驚喜♥
-
Unexpected encounters in life
are all surprises in your efforts ♥

MEI GIRLS × 2020

咪雅

Mia

instagram： @mia2609842

MEI GIRLS × 2020

尤尤

Linda

instagram： @linda.zz99tw

[千辛萬苦，只為與你修成正果 ♥]

MEI GIRLS
2020
Linda

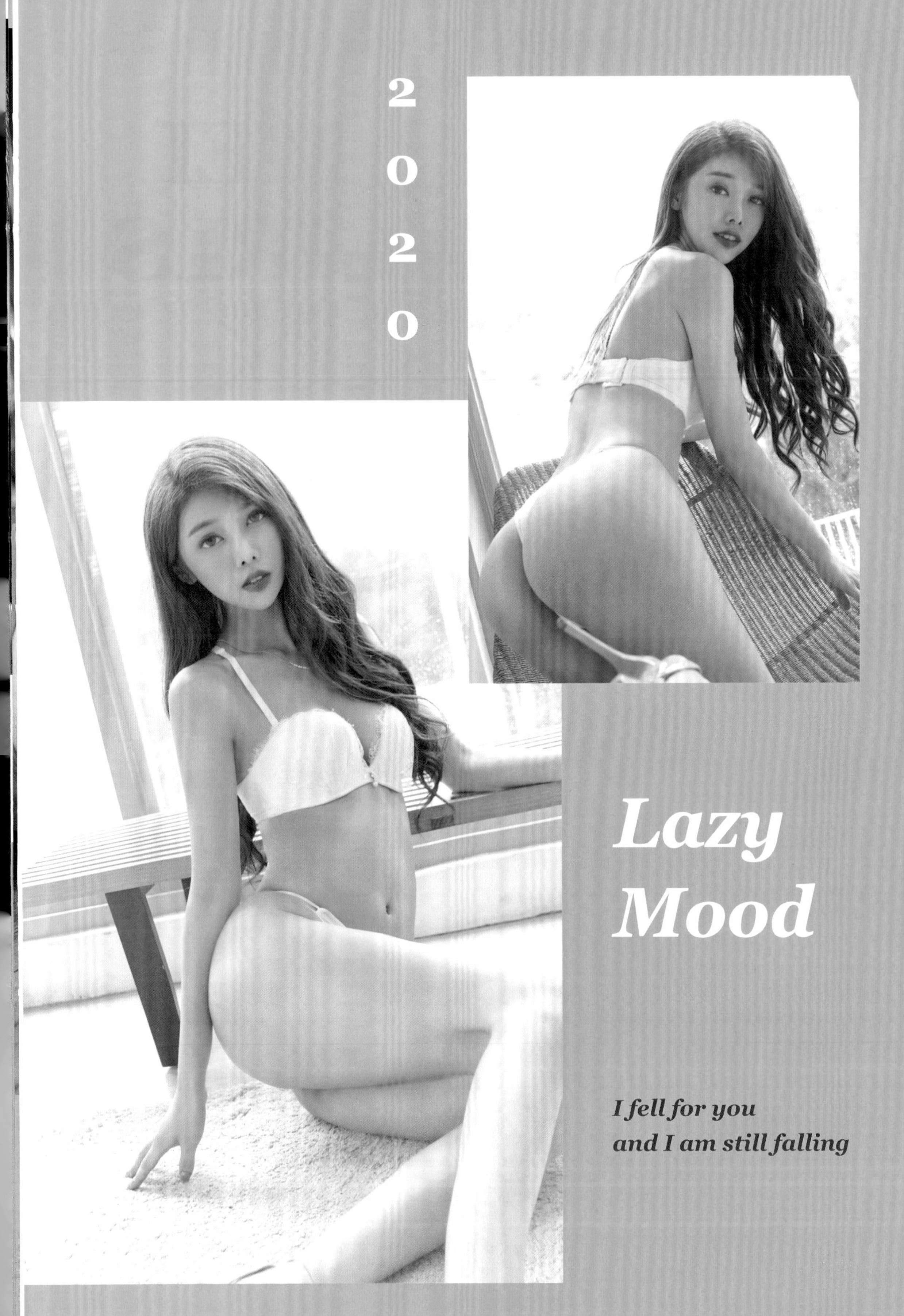

2020

Lazy Mood

I fell for you
and I am still falling

MEI GIRLS × 2020

肝連

Miao

instagram： @miaoo131

月亮不睡我不睡，我是你的小寶貝。

molten

SDARE

Sporty Girl

MEI GIRLS 2020

Miao

-

Summer Breeze

Sporty
Girl
-
Summer Breeze
MEI
GIRLS
2020
Miao
Taiwan Top 100 Girls
Album.

Summer Breeze

天氣很熱沒關係，
你不要對我忽冷忽熱就好了。

MEI GIRLS

2020

木子萱

instagram： @mz1219

Summer
Believe
In
Yourself

Adorable
Taiwan
Top 100 Girls
Album.
-
I long to be a sunflower
a lover of golden light,
a creator of sweet laughter.

2020 年 YouTube 頻道，
努力邁入 20 萬訂閱！

MEI GIRLS × 2020

釣蝦女神系
沐雨柔

instagram： @evemu716

Make Dream Come True

-

I fell for you and I am still falling, you are my new favorite feeling.

MEI GIRLS 2020

2020
Taiwan
Top 100 Girls Album

NOE
246

MEI GIRLS 2020

Summer Vibes

Find joy
in the journey

SUM —
MER
2 0 2 0

Summer

2020

MEI GIRLS × 2020

吳芸帆

Micky

instagram：@mickybaby0611

「現在認識還不算晚，就怕你不來認識我。」

Make Today Magical

-

I'm happy
when
I'm with you

MEI GIRLS 2020

Micky

I'm happy
when I'm with you.

你摸摸我衣服的料子，
是不是做你女朋友的料。

MEI GIRLS × 2020

詩錡

Vicky

instagram： @11.xox.20

MEI GIRLS × 2020

妮

Ginny

instagram： @ginny1213

[愛笑愛鬧，任性也撒嬌♥]

MEI GIRLS 2020
Find
Joy
In The
Journey
-
You are better than all
anything

MEI GIRLS × 2020

焦焦

Jiao

instagram： @jiao_fff

「你追不到我，就追我 IG ♥」

2
0
2
0

MEI GIRLS 2020

Jiao

Taiwan Top 100 Girls
Have
A Nice
Day
-
Wish some days lasted
forever.

Have A Nice Day

-

Wish some days lasted forever.

MEI
GIRLS
2020
Jiao

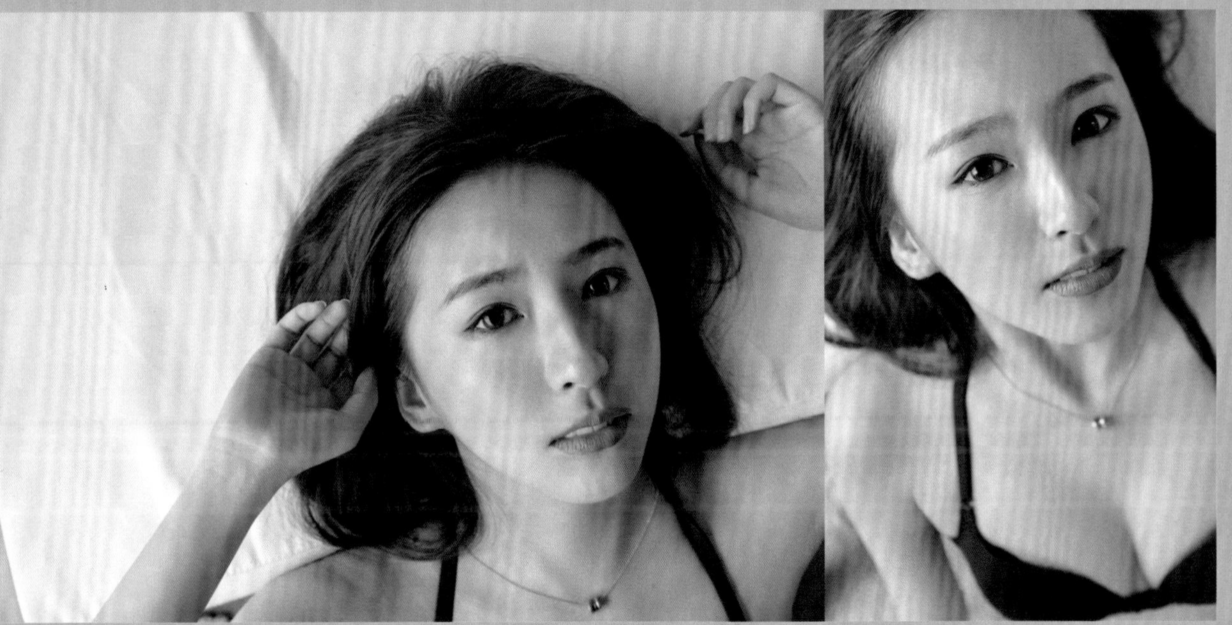

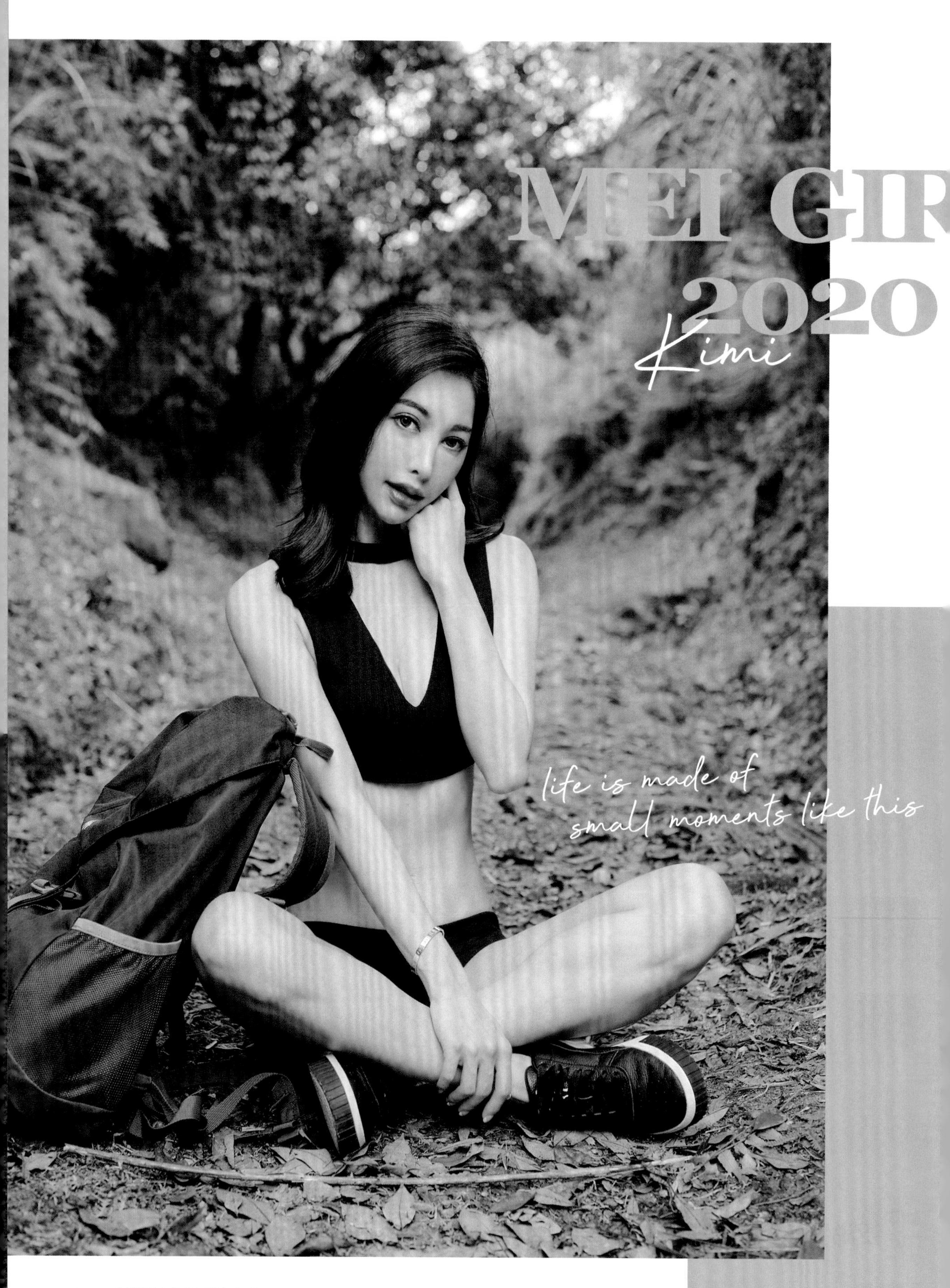
MEI GIR
2020
Kimi
life is made of
small moments like this

S

Stay
Wild
And Free

生活有點苦，不如加點我吧♥

MEI GIRLS × 2020

糖可可

鄭苡玟

instagram：@candyo3o5

Taiwan Top 100 Girls

The best thing to hold onto in life is each other.

2
0
2
0

SPORTHOLIC

-

I'm happy when
I'm with you

Girl Power

SPORTHOLIC

-

I'm happy when
I'm with you

Taiwan Top 100 Girls

2
0
2
0

Girl Power

MEI GIRLS 2020

-

Angel Energy

如果你老是嘴饞，你的 0 食在這♥

MEI GIRLS × 2020

Ling Ling

instagram： @zero_zero_ling

Taiwan
Top 100 Girls Album

MEI GIRLS 2020

Ling Ling

Angel Energy

-

The best thing to hold onto in life is each other.

MEI GIRLS × 2020

stay wild and free

DAYDREAM

-

Dream a little dream of me

Best Memories

-

Dream a little dream
Of me

DAYDREAM

BE

HAPPY

ALWAYS

所有的事情在沒有結果前，
都是播種。

MEI GIRLS × 2020

密寶
張筱密

instagram： @ltmimi

MEI GIRLS × 2020

Closer To Happiness Than I've Ever Been

-

In your life my infinite dreams live.

BE HAPPY

ALWAYS

我等不及想再見到你❤

MEI GIRLS × 2020

雪兒

Michelle

instagram： @michelle19951212

MEI GIRLS 2020

Michelle

Love Is An Adventure

-

**You are my
New favorite feeling.**

Amazing
Love
Is An
Adventure
-
Wish you were here

MEI GIRLS
2020
Michelle

MEI GIRLS

瑄妹兒

instagram： @milk08110811

我可愛也可壞，都是你的人。

POSITIVE.

Summer Vibes

-

Find joy in the journey.

SUM — MER

2 0 2 0

MEI GIRLS 2020

Xuan

SUM —

MER

2 0 2 0

Summer Vibes

-

Find joy in the journey.

2020 好吃的東西要吃進肚子裡，
可愛的人要放在心裡！

MEI GIRLS × 2020

凡凡

instagram： @eyvonne623

MEI GIRLS
2020
belong with you,
belong with me.

I Love Seeing You Happy

-

Closer to happiness
Than I've ever been.

MEI GIRLS × 2020

馮苡珺

instagram：@fengfeng.k

[2020 希望疫情趕快結束大家都平安]

Make
Dream
Come True.
ORIGINAL
SWEET
FLOWERS
dream
BIG
All of me loves
all of you
Love
In
Your
Heart.

2020

MEI
GIRLS
2020

You Are My Adventure

MEI GIRLS × 2020

2020

Make Dream Come True.

-

Love In Your Heart.

用微笑改變這個世界，
別讓這個世界改變你的微笑。

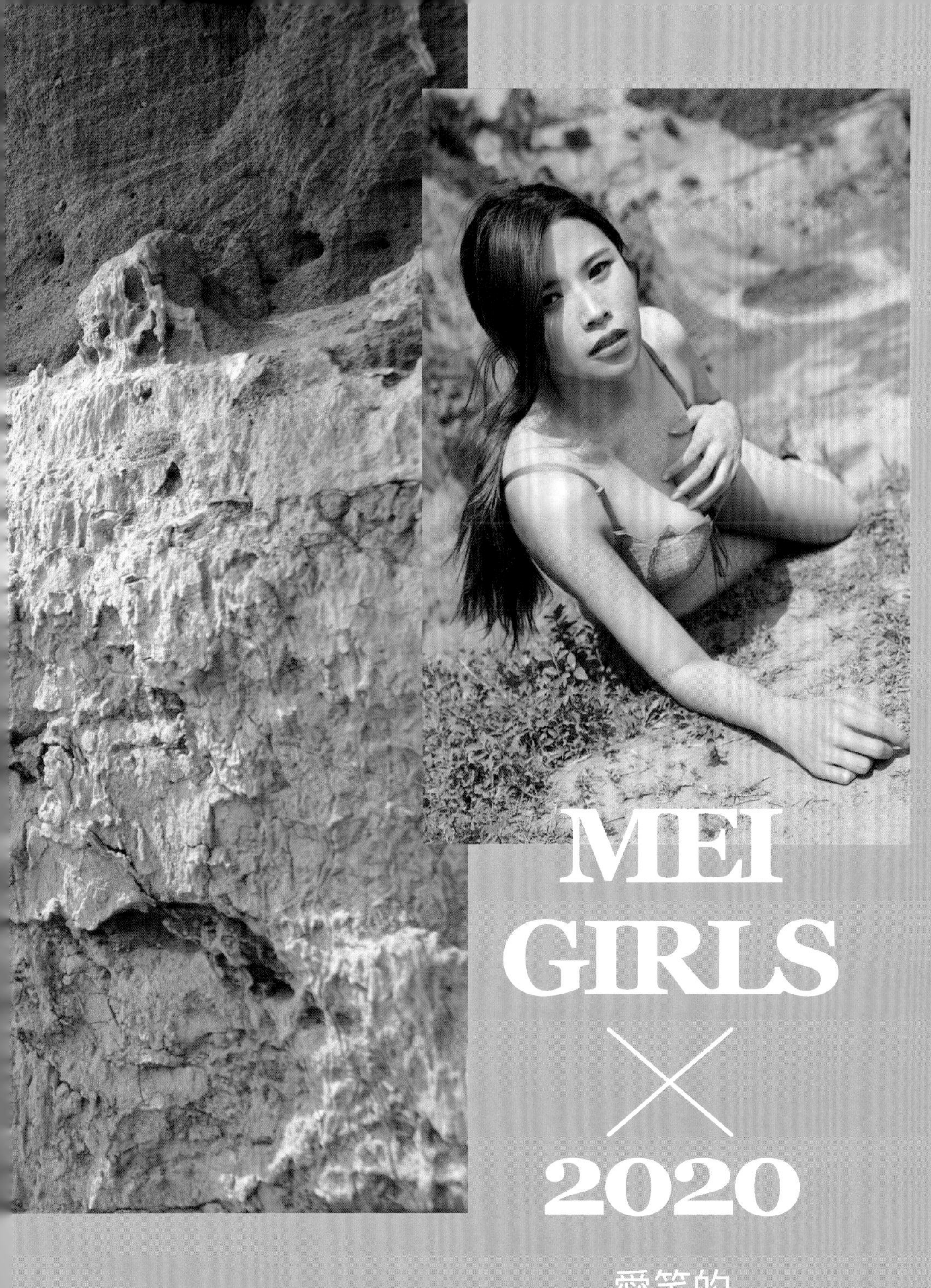

MEI GIRLS × 2020

愛笑的

Alice

instagram： @alicelovevip

MEI GIRLS 2020

Alice

\-

find joy in the journey.

Summertime

-

life is made of
small moments like this.

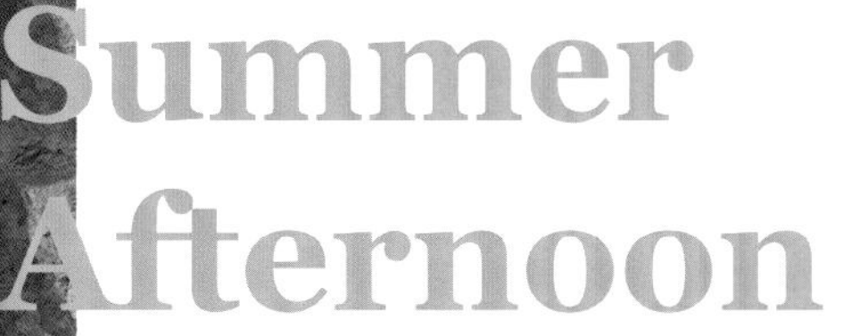

MEI GIRLS
2020

Summer Afternoon

-

life is made of small moments like this.

MEI GIRLS

2020

大D

instagram： @n.930__

快樂的方式很多，
但最直接的方式就是能每天看到你。

MEI GIRLS 2020

La Vie Est Belle

-

You Are My Adventure.

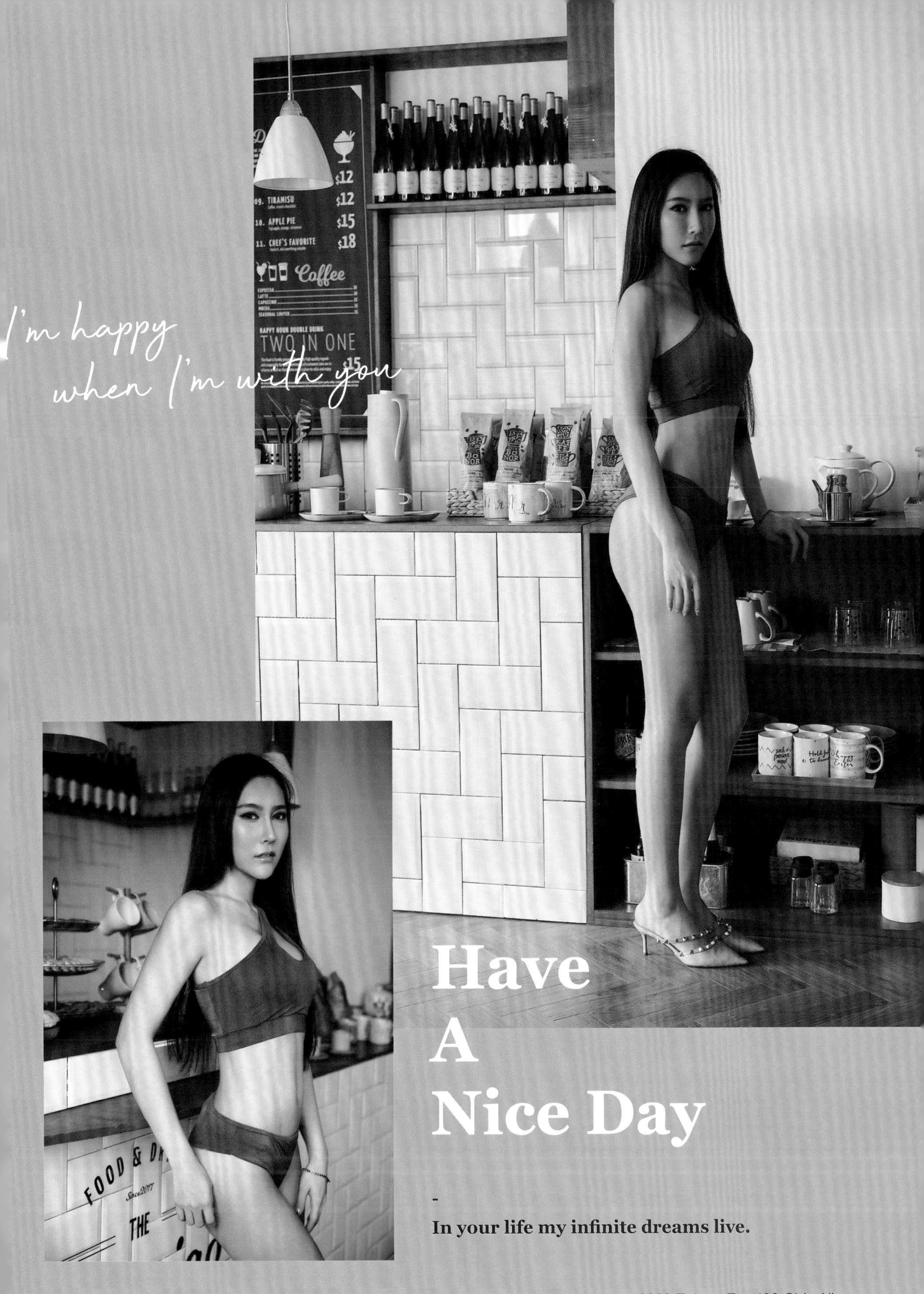

09. TIRAMISU $12
10. APPLE PIE $15
11. CHEF'S FAVORITE $18
Coffee
TWO IN ONE
I'm happy
when I'm with you
Have
A
Nice Day
-
In your life my infinite dreams live.

Have
A
Nice Day

-

In your life my infinite dreams live.

MEI GIRLS 2020

I'm happy when I'm with you

-

In your life my infinite dreams live.

MEI GIRLS × 2020

凱拉

Kyra

instagram： @kyra.528

「珍惜每個特別的相遇包括你們。」

MEI GIRLS 2020

Kyra

-

You are better than all anything

Sunset Girl

-

I long to be a sunflower,
a lover of golden light,
a creator of sweet laughter.

All of me loves
all of you

Sunset Girl

-

You are better than all anything

I long to be a sunflower,
a lover of golden light,
a creator of sweet laughter.

書　　名｜2020 台灣百大網紅聯名寫真
總 編 輯｜陳豪
副 編 輯｜沈琪琪
發行單位｜名媚國際股份有限公司
企劃團隊｜紅紅數位股份有限公司
協力單位｜捷喜多媒體數位股份有限公司
熱浪新媒體股份有限公司
攝影團隊｜ Zhuo Zheng Song Photo Studio
美編設計｜ B.H Studio
整體造型｜ FF Fashion Styling Studio
特別感謝｜ S'dare Sport
印　　數｜二冊精裝套書
出版年月｜ 2020 年 9 月
I S B N ｜ 978-986-99582-0-2

定價－新台幣 1580 元